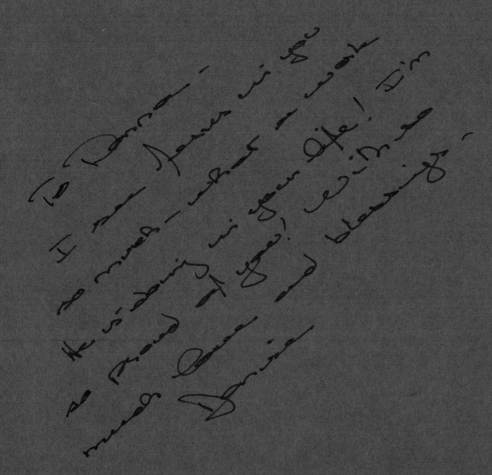

and the ROCKS CRY OUT

Encounters with our Living God

By a Sister on Her Journey Home
DENISE ZAPFFE PARK

The crowds were blessing and cheering Jesus as He rode into Jerusalem on a donkey in triumph. The Pharisees told Jesus that He should keep his followers quiet. Jesus replied, "I tell you that, if these should hold their peace, the stones would immediately cry out." Luke 19:40 KJV

Copyright © 2005 Denise Z. Park
www.churchestellstory.com

Denise Z. Park is also the editor of the book *Our Churches Tell the Story*, © 2004

First published in the
United States by:
Evergreen Press of Brainerd, LLC.
201 West Laurel Street
P.O. Box 465
Brainerd, MN 56401
(218) 828-6424
www.evergreenpress.org

ISBN 978-0-9755252-1-0
Printed in the United States of America

Photography and Text:
Denise Z. Park

Project Management:
Chip Borkenhagen

Design:
Mandi Yliniemi

Editor:
Tenlee Lund

Color Management:
Bryan Petersen

*T*o my beloved daughter, Jeanie, who after a few short years of life, died

and left me with many questions about God, life, purpose and suffering.

I will never forget her blue eyes and impish ways. In death, my God used

her to show me truth and a way back to Him – a real gift to me. I give

thanks and expect to see her in heaven with my Jesus.

*A*ll of these photographs are my own, except for four family shots. They have been taken with a small automatic camera in eleven countries and seventeen states. Many have been taken in state and national parks, especially on my 14,000-mile car trip, alone, around the western U.S. The rest are from my travels and my everyday photo collection. I did not label them for the reason that they are symbols for the companion words.

This book was mainly thought of and written in 1995, predating my stained glass window book, *Our Churches Tell the Story*. It has been on my heart to complete this ever since. I have redone this whole book in six months. It is a very personal journal, not a Bible.

TO THE READER

*I*f you were to travel to a foreign country, you would find it to your advantage to learn its language and customs in order to fit in and find favor with the people and their king. This is like our relation to the Bible and to our God. He is definitely alive and well!

It is a crazy world we live in today. Science has all the answers. Books on "spiritual porn" (witchcraft) and its usage are "in." The stars have answers and guidance. What feels good, do it. Seek your own truth. He who has the biggest toys wins. You have got to pull yourself up by your own boot straps. Love yourself. Esteem goes to actors, athletes, and intellectuals. Gold rules. These are some of today's worldly concepts. These do not answer the call of our inmost being or fill our heart with peace. There is a void in each of us – and that can be filled only by God, Himself. I have tried many ways. In desperation I finally discovered where answers can be found – in our Maker's manual, the Bible. All else is either worldly fluff or counterfeit. Without a deep faith, life is a charade waiting for or

avoiding its end. I do not want to come to the end of my life on earth in anger and fear, as my parents did, but once again want to fly into the arms of my Jesus, whom I had met in a near-death experience. Then I knew that I never would find such a consuming love on earth – and I was angry to have to return.

There is nothing in life that has not already happened to God's people in the Bible. Tragedies, life's exigencies, or stress may make us want to escape, but an encounter with Jesus Christ demands a response. A "yes" opens up a new world of living in God's presence. I honor Him for lovingly and gently revealing Himself to me through His creation, though making it clear that nothing in His creation should be idolized. Instead, I let these blessings and revelations lure me into intimacy with Him. This book shows that there are many things in God's creation which reflect heaven. Look for them in your own life!

I may seem bold to some, but I fearfully am trying to do my best in being truthful and honest. First and foremost, I desire to honor God and thank Him for His loving care and patience with me. In doing this book as an artistic creation, my heart has become even more enraptured with Him.

I have a desire to mold myself into the words He has whispered to me, especially in the last three chapters. So this book, in a manner of speaking, is revealing Him to you, the reader. You might ask, "How do I hear God?" Actually, I have heard His voice only twice in my life – once to tell me that my present husband was "a gift," when I had no intentions of remarrying. This journal, outside of being experiential, is what we today might call a "download" of knowing. Since my mind is rather hardened by experience, God places symbols or scripture right in front of my face. Then I "dream." I give thanks to His Holy Spirit for so much revelation. Please be assured that I am not "there" yet, since I am awesomely human! I know where I have been – but now I know Whose I am. His words are my hope toward which I aim my heart.

I pray that you, the reader, are on this path – the one where our Father meets you where you are. Life, for me, has never been the same since I have allowed my heart to call out to Him, to allow Him to woo and captivate me. His Holy Spirit makes His Word and promises leap off the pages of the Bible. These words are changing my mind and give my heart a hunger for more.

Living is all about Him and His Son. Period.

—Denise Z. Park

INTRODUCTION

*T*his is my story. It can be anybody's story from youth to a compulsive misdirected life with bad choices and the results from those choices. Life can have its share of tragedies, which can derail us, unless we have a foundation in what our Creator ordained when He made us.

This book is about victory, not tragedy. My Dad gave me a fascination with cosmic mysteries, but no foundation to prepare me for handling immense grief and pain through loss – the death of my child caused by my own negligence. After many years in a dark season of life, with only a speck of faith that Jesus was leading me somewhere, I have been made new. I am experiencing more and more of our Father's love and blessings, as well as His grieving heart over those who are lost and far from Him – and the urgency called for in these fearful times. He longs to draw us close to Him, but our minds and hearts shut Him out. Our spirits are His and they should be free to be with Him.

In my church circles, I had always envied and skeptically questioned how people heard from God. I had felt more despondent and rejected when I never did hear Him . . . until I took up hiking in parks. Then, all of a sudden and to my immense joy, a gentle voice came from rocks, trees, and other simple things. This voice actually answered my questions! It had never occurred to me to LOOK where God might be. He can speak through symbols all around us. I felt like a child once again, rediscovering the joys of new sight, while running and dancing with released abandon in the presence of my God! I have seen many years of life, but with His Spirit in me, those years fell away to leave me just as I am – my Father's child, precious, innocent, and free through His Son, Jesus. To realize how I am held precious in God's eyes and loved by Him, means that you are, too. After my many wrong choices in life, I find this amazing! He is a God of second chances! Subsequently, His Spirit is leading me, giving me the strength and gifts needed to reach out to others in this needy world.

In 1995 I started this book while hiking with a small notebook and a camera. Many of the observations and answers to my questions, posed to the Almighty, were written down and lovingly put into a collection along with companion photos. This book is an expanded and more mature version. Most of the time, I had not known what page or photo would go next. But God did. One just has to listen. I have tried to keep each phrase true to the character of God as found in the included scripture references. I do not claim to be perfect, but have tried to keep what I have heard and written in line with His Word in the Bible.

Will you expectantly walk with me and hear God's voice through these pages and be encouraged? He is ever near, even in the simple things in life. I sincerely pray that this journal will enrich your walk with our Father-Creator and give you a deeper revelation of who He is. Amen.

—Denise Park

SEASONS
of My Life

To every thing there is a season, and a time to every purpose under the heaven. Ecclesiastes 3:1 KJV

A TAPESTRY *of* HOPE

A shuttle guided by higher hands
Weaves threads back and forth in colored strands;
Some are glimmering silver and gold,
Others murky brown and black so bold
Giving depth and definition to my fine cloth –
These strands of sorrowful tears and joy aloft.

Many people have come into my life;
Some to bring love, others painful strife,
Yet each contributes their special strand
Toward completing a picture so grand
With the warp being mine given at birth,
The woof created as time marches on earth.

What the picture is, I do not know –
It is hard to see from here below
But I observe and learn from each stitch.
At times I rise on a higher pitch
And exclaim, "Oh, my goodness, what a show!"
As I see the pattern take shape below.

The picture is not all complete
But what I see is ever so neat
As the brighter threads lighten the dark,
What I thought was hopeless, now gives the spark
To forgive myself and others for deeds done –
It has been a long battle but feel that I've won.

Denise Park 1984

✝
10

THE INVITATION
The Journey Begins

*A*nd ye shall know the truth, and the truth shall make you free.   John 8:32 KJV

I am the LORD, your God, calling you, My beloved child. I am here! I long for you to come into My Presence so I can reveal My love and touch your heart.

Exodus 20:3, 1 John 3:1, Psalm 16:11

$\mathcal{B}$e still and listen to My voice. Do not be afraid, for I will comfort you. Let My truth, majesty, and especially My love reflect in the well of your opening heart.

Psalms 46:10, 84:5-7, 96:4-6, Isaiah 41:13

$\mathcal{Y}$es, My dearest child – I have revealed Myself to you at death's door in lighted splendor. I have let you feel the incomparable love I have for you, and how I accept you exactly as you are. Let Me show you how your life has been a journey back home to Me.

Matthew 17:1-2, John 3:16

*L*isten, as I gently pour truth and life into every fiber of your being. With great joy, I shall watch you soak it up, as you begin to live in Me. People may have failed you, but I never will forsake you. I love you!

Proverbs 2:1-6, Psalms 63:3, 100:5, Joshua 1:5

Come, My weary one. I yearn for you to come near to Me for I am a God full of mercy. I am ready to receive and abundantly pardon you! Let go of that which has kept you from Me.

John 12:32, Isaiah 55:7,
Nehemiah 9:17, Hebrews 12:1

*M*y child – come to Me as to your Father and rest in Me. Your future may seem unclear, but I will tenderly hold you in My hand as I show you My wisdom and plans for your life.

Hebrews 4:11, Isaiah 49:16,
Proverbs 2:1-6, 20:24

$\mathcal{M}$y precious little one – do not be trapped or cling to the vain and dark thoughts of your mind, which sets itself against Me. Humble yourself before Me and I will lovingly lift you up onto the high Rock, which is My Son, Jesus.

James 4:10, Romans 8:7,
1 Corinthians 10:4, Colossians 2:8-9

*B*ecause of My love for you, I gave My Son, who came into the world, stretched out His arms, and died for you on a cross. He bore your sins and reaped your punishment. He gave all that He had. He is the door to your salvation and eternal life in Me – where your real journey begins.

John 3:16, 10:9, Colossians 1:20-22, Hebrews 9:12, Isaiah 53:4-7

$\mathcal{M}$y cherished one – I have gently opened this door for you to come out of your darkened house. I have longed to bring you into a world of light and truth. I will free you! I lead My sheep to green pastures by springs of life-giving water. Take My hand and choose to come on this journey with Me.

John 1:4, Isaiah 49:9-10, Matthew 16:24

$\mathcal{M}$y Son, Jesus, is alive and longs to be your Friend, Husband, and Lord. He has paid for you with His blood and claims you for My very own. He is the One who has been knocking on the door of your heart. Let Him in! Believe in Him!

John 15:14, 20:28,30-31, Isaiah 54:5, Hebrews 9:12, Revelation 3:20

$\mathcal{A}$s you open your door of belief in My Son, We will award you with Our Holy Spirit as proof of Our ownership, acceptance, and forgiveness. He will remain with you to prepare a holy place for Us to come and live with you. You are now born into real living!

2 Corinthians 1:21-22, Ephesians 1:13-14

*W*hen you choose to come under Our authority ask Our Holy Spirit, or have a sister pray with you, to light this match which starts the fire of My amazing gifts to flow through you. You will feel His Presence and a new empowerment to live! Your spirit will sparkle with Our joy! You will have a new understanding of My Word and an interactive relationship with Me through My Son, Jesus – your Savior and Redeemer.

Acts 2:1-4, John 16:7-15, 1 Corinthians 2:10-14

$\mathcal{M}$y Spirit will be your conscience and comforter. He is gentle. He will lead you and show you how to stay on the narrow path which My Son, Jesus, tells you about. This path will lead you away from worldly living into My heart and a full life, with which I want to bless you.

1 John 2:27, Proverbs 4:25-27,
Matthew 7:13-14, 11:29, Jeremiah 24:7

$\mathcal{M}$y chosen one – My heart urgently calls yours to learn to live fully in My Son, Jesus. Apart from Him, you can do nothing! On this journey, Our Spirit will lead you up steps into My Kingdom that will try you. It may be difficult, but I have ordered your steps and given you swift feet.

John 15:5, Psalms 18:32-33,36, 37:23-24, Habakkuk 3:19

$\mathcal{I}$ will break the chains which conform and enslave you to the world's gods and ways of selfish thinking. These hold you back from My light and a full life. I will show you the truth and you will be free!

Ephesians 2:1-3, Luke 4:18, John 8:32, 10:10

My treasured one – open doors between us bring you into My garden of delights. I have created you to walk with Me in My garden. I long for you to live in My Presence under the branches of My Tree of Eternal Life. There you will have no fears and can delight in Me as I delight in you! Psalm 37:4, Genesis 3:3, 8

$\mathcal{M}$y little one – see the butterflies? Come away from drinking stagnant water when your spirit is reborn and new in Me. Choose life in My holy Presence, not spiritual death. Come and drink from Me!

John 3:3, 4:13-14, Deuteronomy 30:19

*L*et go of those fears ruling your life and all things from the past which are dead and keep you far from me. Receive My forgiveness and walk by faith – not by what you see or feel.

2 Timothy 1:7, Philippians 3:13, Isaiah 59:2, 2 Corinthians 5:7

$\mathcal{M}$y loved one – like this lily whose feet are sunk deep into the mud, you had sunk into sin. See, I have called you to reach out to Me with your whole heart.   Psalm 25:7, 1 John 1:7, Isaiah 54:7

$\mathcal{L}$et my light expose and dispel all darkness, sin, and what is unholy in
you. As you come out of this mud through the pure cleansing water of
My Word to Me, your spirit will be born into a new life in My Kingdom.
You will be beautiful! I do this because I love you beyond mere words.

John 1:12-13, 8:12, Acts 22:16, Ephesians 5:26

$\mathcal{M}$y chosen one – there have been rough times while letting your will line up with Mine – choosing Me as your God over your own self. These were lessons in your overcoming the world to live in My Kingdom. James 1:12, Romans 7:14-25, Revelation 3:21

$\mathcal{T}$here have been many wildernesses in your life. My Son, Jesus, has been there, too. It is where My chosen people find Me when they cry out. Listen and give thanks for a Father who cares for you!

Matthew 4:1-11, Deuteronomy 29:1-15, Psalm 50:15, 1 Peter 5:7

*Y*es, My broken one – come to Me as a child who crawls onto his father's lap to feel comfort and security. I see your tears and I tenderly record each one in my book. Weeping may last for a night, but there will be joy in the morning! Psalms 30:5, 56:8, 144:2

*M*y beloved creation – I found you helpless, naked, and cast aside. I lovingly picked you up, wrapped you in My cloak to cover you, and called you by name to live. You are not a disposable item, but precious to Me! Now I will give you the finest things and make a covenant with you, binding you to Me as in a marriage. Ezekiel 16:6-13

𝓘 will wipe away every tear from your eyes and carry you close to
My heart. There will be no more pain or sorrow, for I shall give you My
peace that passes all understanding and a refreshing in the waters of life.

Revelation 21:4, Isaiah 40:11, Philippians 4:7, Acts 3:19, Psalm 84:5-6

$\mathcal{C}$ome near to Me, My beloved child. Just "living" your life is only a shadow of the life you will have in Me. I will keep you as the apple of My eye. There are more lessons to learn. John 10:10,28, James 4:8, Psalm 17:8

*M*y dearest child – I see into the windows of your soul that you are beginning to long for My waters of eternal life. Do not doubt, but believe! I can remove those mountains in the way. Only ask.

Revelation 21:6, Mark 11:23-24

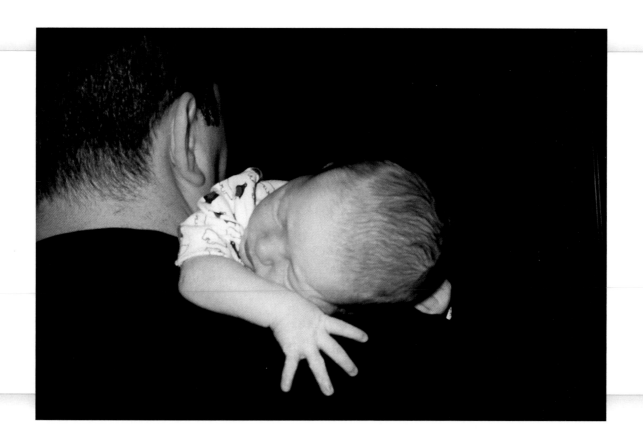

$\mathcal{B}$elieve that I am your Father who loves you with an everlasting love.

I will carry you through life and on this journey ahead.

Jeremiah 31:3, Isaiah 40:11

$\mathcal{C}$ome, my little one. Follow Me. Be a trusting and obedient lamb – not
a rebellious goat. I will gently draw you with bands of love, and I will
heal your wounds.   Exodus 19:5, Hosea 6:1-3, 11:4

$\mathcal{G}$oats have a lazy, stubborn nature and go their own way, tending to their own needs. The sheep will follow the Good Shepherd; the goats will be separated from Me.   John 10:9,27-30, Matthew 25:31-46

*G*oats, at the end of their lives, will feel like potsherd or dried clay –
angry and bitter over what they could never control. How could they
feel received by Me? Psalm 22:15, Proverbs 16:25, John 14:6

I will lead you by still waters to restore you. I am delighted that you hear My call. All of My company in heaven are rejoicing! Let the lifeless things flow away.   Psalm 23:2-3, 34:15, Luke 15:7, 1 Peter 4:3

$\mathcal{M}$y precious child – I will show you a place to worship Me in the beauty of My holiness. Set time aside to speak to Me from your own heart, where I reside.   Psalm 29:2, Jeremiah 24:7, John 14:23

$\mathcal{I}$ will set you among people who love My Son, Jesus, and honor Him as Lord over their lives. See how they reflect His love by loving one another? John 13:35, Ephesians 4:1-6, Psalm 2:11-12

I see trust and longing in your eyes. I also long for you. All in heaven are celebrating that you are going on this journey with me! I will not leave you nor forsake you.

Psalm 84:2, Luke 15:7, Deuteronomy 31:8

I have heard your cries to Me. I will lead you with grace, mercy, and love on a journey to heal your wounds, to tear down your strongholds, and to lead you to become the person I have created you to be. Put your hand in Mine and listen attentively with your heart, mind, and soul. Let us begin!

Proverbs 2:1-6, Psalms 100:5, 63:3

TO MY DAUGHTER *Jean* (1965-69)

Little one, born of my flesh and blood –
Where would you be today if you were here?
But no, you left me alone in a flood
Of tears and remorse as I tried to bring cheer
To others missing you but neglected my wounds within
Which festered and bled throughout the years
Till I found myself all alone with a heavy burden
Of the sins committed to escape my fears
Of more loved ones being ripped from my care,
Leaving me isolated and alone in a place
Far from home in a desert bare
Of songs and laughter, love or a happy face.

How I miss you, my daughter of love and grace,
My blue-eyed imp of joy and spontaneity –
Am I guilty of letting you live such a short space
Denying us the pleasure of seeing you to maturity,
Or did you come to bless those who followed you
By creating a priority that little ones are the best
O'er the world's delusions and trappings that pursue
One relentlessly away from his duty and joy in the nest?
I am angry that this car accident left us so bereft
At a time when we'd never tasted the bitter dregs of death,
But, my own dear child, I send you better words
    than when you left –
Thank you for your brief visit, the love on your dying breath.

Denise Park 1984

SEASON 1
A Life's Descent

*A*ll of us have strayed away like sheep. We have left God's paths to follow our own. Yet the LORD laid on Him (Jesus) the guilt and sins of us all.

Isaiah 53:6 NLT

My y precious child – I am your Creator.
I formed you in secret and covered you in
your mother's womb. You are wonderfully
made and I am pleased with My work.

Genesis 1:27,31, Psalm 139:13,15

I lovingly covered and protected you under My wings, caressing you with My feathers, as I wove your inward parts together.   Psalms 91:4, 139:14-15

I apportioned gifts for you to use to bless others. I made plans for your

life to give you a future and a hope. Romans 12:3-8, Jeremiah 29:11

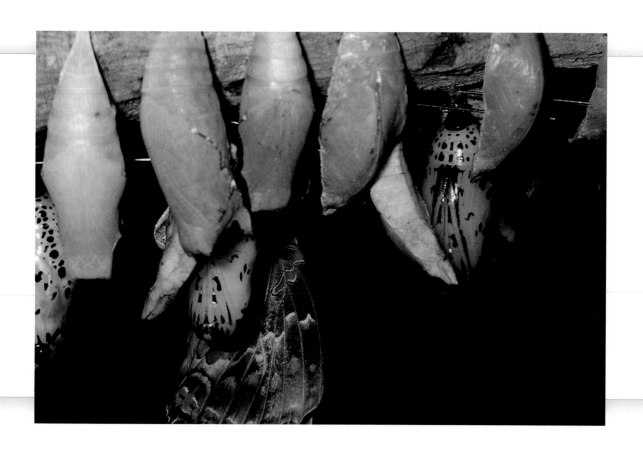

I tenderly brought you into the world as my beautiful child of promise,

set apart for Me. Isaiah 40:11, Romans 9:8

I clothed you with skin and flesh and knit your bones and sinews together. I gave you life and showed you My favor and unfailing care.

Job 10:11-12

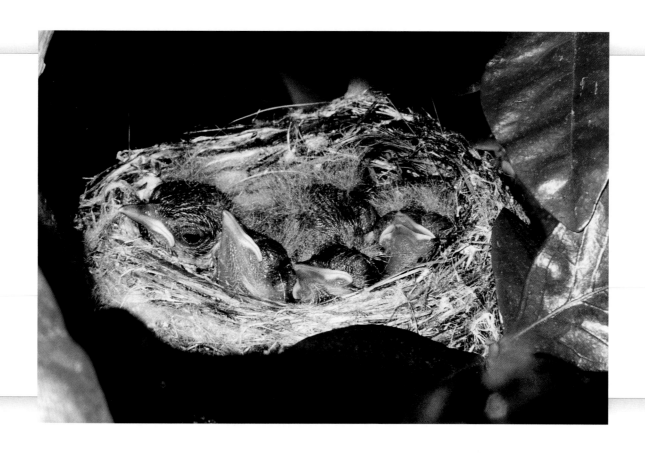

$\mathcal{I}$, Myself, stooped down to feed you because I care for you with an everlasting love. Hosea 11:3-4, Jeremiah 31:3

*L*ike this child, I rejoiced when I saw you dance before Me, with joy over My gifts to you and in the beauty of My creation.

Psalm 149:3, 2 Samuel 6:14

$\mathcal{Y}$ou loved your parents. You tried to be super perfect. You were just a child as I watched you try so hard to please them by sharing the responsibility of seven more children. Your life in Me was being shut off by this effort and their weaknesses.

Matthew 11:28-30, 13:22

You grew into a beautiful young woman –
a precious possession of Mine as I hovered
over you. Psalm 17:8

$\mathcal{T}$hrough your parents I gave you the riches of the world, but I am your Father who has eternal riches. I will lead you with ropes of love and kindness into the Kingdom of My Presence – the source of your peace and joy.

Ecclesiastes 5:19, Ephesians 2:1-10,
Hosea 11:3-4, Romans 14:17

$\mathcal{I}$ watched you glide into life, relying on your spirit and desires. You were strong and determined, seeking truths with your mind. You were not given a good foundation in Me.   Proverbs 14:12, 1 Corinthians 3:10-11

I grieved for you when you forgot Me and My commands. You preferred to enjoy the excitement of your youth. My light began to disappear in your life. Genesis 6:6, Ecclesiastes 12:1, John 1:1-5

You became bent to the ways of the world – filling that place for Me with unholy things.

Proverbs 16:25, 1 Corinthians 6:19

$\mathcal{Y}$our journey has to go under the arms of My Son, Jesus, who paid the ransom for you on the cross. There is no other way. You can have only one Master. You cannot serve Me and worldly material things at the same time.

1 Corinthians 6:20, Matthew 6:24, John 14:6, Acts 4:10-12

I was there when you made a covenant of marriage with your mate. After four years of waiting, I saw your relief that you were able to finally show the world that your love and intentions were real.   Matthew 19:4-6

I blessed you with seven beautiful and healthy children. I was with you through their milestones, as well as their illnesses and accidents. But I was not invited into your marriage. Psalm 127:3-5, John 2:1-11

*Y*our daughter has died. I am holding you closer than ever. You will find comfort in My arms, close to My heart. I am using this tragedy to grow compassion in your heart for others and to change your priorities. I am showing you the value of children, which is how I feel about you. She is a sign in your life – pointing the way back to Me.

John 14:6, Romans 8:28

*M*y broken child – remember My Son, Jesus, saying that He would be with you through this calamity when you met Him last year? Your tears are My tears. Heaven mourns with you. Your altar in the world is broken. I want to hear your voice crying out to Me and I will come to enfold you with my comfort and love.

Ezekiel 6:6, Psalms 36:7, 72:12,
2 Corinthians 1:3

*M*y beloved child – I am holding your bleeding heart in My hand. You are so dear to Me! If only you would know Me, I could heal you and bring you peace.

Hosea 2:20, Exodus 15:26, Psalm 4:8

I have your daughter with Me. I have shown you how she delights in playing with Me. This is not only a time to allow others to comfort you, but a time of testing who you are, your faith, and if you trust Me. I promised to be with you always – not that your life will go your way. I ask you to read My Word in your Bible, which shows you how to live life and how to know Me, your Creator.

James 1:2-7, Psalm 119:33-40, Joshua 1:9

$\mathscr{B}$ut now I sadly watch your faith and life go up in flames as you settle into grief and self-blame. Psalm 31:10

You ou will now be in a wintertime of your soul, yet I will continue to call you to Me.

Psalm 31:9, Jeremiah 31:3

$\mathcal{O}$h, dearest child – I see you walking away from Me. Do you choose your own wilderness rather than a life with Me? Your daughter's death is not a judgment on you, like your earthly father said, nor My rejection of you. That is not why My Son, Jesus, came. Psalm 103:6, John 12:47

*D*o you think that your self-made prison will be safe? You are hiding behind your pride, thinking that others will see a person of strength. I see you bury your grief inside and deny your need of Me or anyone else. If only you would call to Me to deliver you!

Psalm 10:4, Ecclesiastes 2:23, Jeremiah 33:3

$\mathscr{S}$peak to Me, My child! I long for you! I am grieving that you are becoming a skeleton in a desert. You are wasting your life – the gift I have given you.

Psalms 78:40, 102:3-7, John 1:9

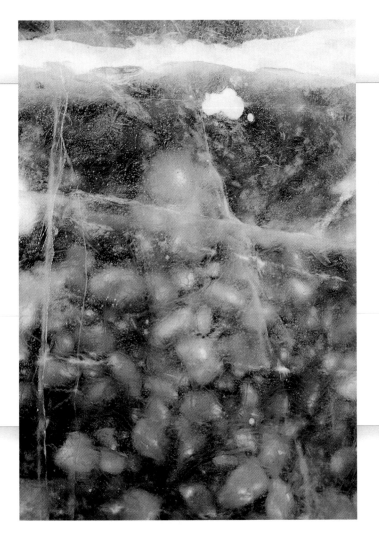

*D*ear one – look how hope has frozen in you. Your spirit is crying out for Me as your life is ebbing away.   Psalm 42:3,6

I sadly see your rejection and anger at Me, your Father and Creator.

You are building walls in your life to keep Me out.

Jonah 4:1, Ephesians 4:26-27, 1 Samuel 10:19

*S*ince you have rejected Me, I will depart from you for a season until you seek Me. I would hold you close to protect you from the evil one in the world. I will wait for your call.

Jeremiah 8:9, Hosea 5:6, Matthew 6:13, Psalms 50:15, 57:1

A Desert

I feel like a lone wanderer in this god-forsaken land –
A desert full of stickers and prickers where no one
    lends a hand.
I desperately reach out to show others that I care
But they turn away and pretend that I am not there.
Hatred and malice spring up like thorns everywhere,
Scourging and scratching in places of which I am unaware.
Where is the Light that turns this breath of wrath away?
I yearn for His Presence, which seems to have
    departed today.

My limbs, limp with the dry wind, sway as it blows,
As I cry and die for love, it rips and tears my clothes.
All alone amidst this roar of silence is no life worth living;
We are humans who grow and learn by taking and giving.
Let me rise and flee from this land so dry and wasted
Where there is no fresh water but only gall to be tasted.
Its very dryness scorches and withers my tormented soul
Like robbers and thieves, keeping me from reaching
    my goal.

Denise Park 1983

SEASON 2
A Life Without God

There is a way that seems right to a man,

but its end is the way of death.

Proverbs 14:12 NKJV

$\mathcal{M}$y dearest child – let us look back on your life when you were angry at Me for twenty years. Losing your daughter was a tragedy that happened to you in a broken world. I had allowed this to happen so that you might know Me, your Father, who loves you. Your children are Mine to give and take. You needed to find truth and life, which is in My Son, Jesus.

Psalms 37:8, 127:3, Job 1:21, John 14:6

*M*y child – if you had given your burdens to Me, I would have given you peace from your pain. You would have found rest and wisdom. I am your Father, the source of all comfort and mercy, who helps you in difficult times.

Philippians 4:7, Psalm 55:22,
2 Corinthians 1:3-4

*Y*ou denied yourself the opportunity to grieve because you felt both rejected by Me and a failure in caring for your child. I am the one who gives you hope and turns your mourning into joyful dancing.

Psalms 30:11, 42:5

*M*y miracle of creation – you chose death rather than life, until you understood that you were insulting Me, your Creator, who was trying to do a good work in you.   Proverbs 8:30, Deuteronomy 30:15, Philippians 1:6

*M*y precious child – you were so beautiful, but so full of pride and rebellion against Me. You did not want to hear My instruction or direction. You thought that you were strong enough to ignore your grief and not let your feelings show.

Deuteronomy 31:27,
Jeremiah 13:15-17, 17:23, Psalm 31:23

$\mathscr{Y}$ou became a fortress of frozen pain, a citadel of frozen perfection. If you had called to Me, I would have answered you. I would have been with you in your troubles and delivered you from despair, which was beginning to consume you.

Psalms 24:9, 91:14-16

$\mathcal{D}$ear one – I watched your husband grieve as he worked harder and found comfort in business relationships. He never knew Me. By his own efforts, he did his best in his concern for earthly gain.

John 1:10, Psalm 17:4, Luke 18:25

*M*oney was his focus, the god he served, as it is with many others. Wealth and false religion can be thieves that destroy any relationship with Me. One finds the fulfillment and joy, which they are looking for, by believing in My Son, Jesus.

Matthew 6:24, Psalm 62:10, John 10:10

*D*earest child – I held you as you looked out on a world where the light seemed to have disappeared. No path seemed right to you. Confusion, loneliness, and despair settled into your torn soul. John 1:9, Jeremiah 3:25

*L*ike knives, these dark thoughts cut you off from Me. Your fear and
hopelessness brought a whirlwind of distress and anguish upon you.
And I was near to be a shelter and a refuge for you!

Proverbs 1:24-28, Psalms 9:9, 72:12

*M*y lost child – how I grieved when I saw you lose your moorings in Me. You lost the hope and any foundation you had in My Son, Jesus. He is the strong and trustworthy anchor of your soul in Me.

Isaiah 33:23, 1 Corinthians 3:11, Hebrews 6:19

$\mathcal{Y}$ou became like a house on shifting sands with no sure foundation. When the floods came later, your house did not stand. Luke 6:46-49

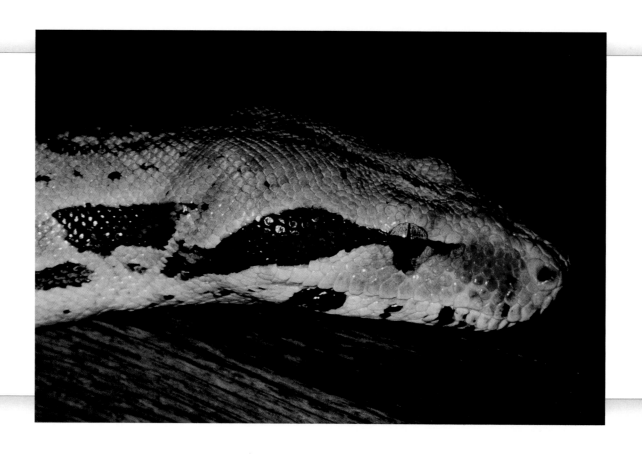

*O*h, My child – your disobedience opened you to the enemy of your soul, who deceived you. He gave you temptations that you could not bear without Me.   Titus 3:3, Psalm 143:3, Ephesians 4:14, 1 Corinthians 10:13

𝒮atan knew how to destroy you. He saw your need for understanding, attention, affirmation, and forgiveness. He brought you into the garden of sexual delights, where you let him tempt and deceive your mind and body. Matthew 10:28, 1 Peter 5:8, 1 John 2:16

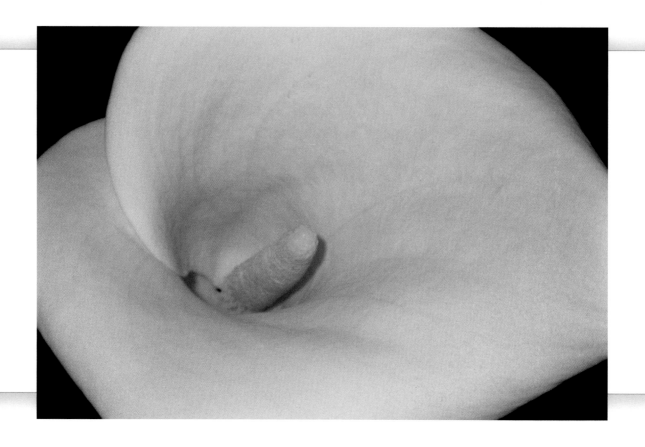

*D*ear child – you traded your white garments in your marriage for those of adulterous shame. You chose death, while trying to kill the pain of your loss and what you thought was My rejection.

Revelation 3:4, Exodus 20:14, Deuteronomy 30:15-16

$\mathcal{Y}$ou played the part of a harlot, fornicating with men, and deserted Me. Your pride, shame, and desire for death were greater than any love you had for Me. Your steps began to go down to the grave. Why didn't you call out to Me? Ezekiel 16:15, Hosea 4:12, 18, Proverbs 5:3-6, Psalm 50:15

$\mathcal{M}$y lost child – I watched your marriage become a lie and die, one piece at a time. What I had blessed became a trap for you and a mask, which you showed to the world. Proverbs 5:15-17, Romans 1:18

*O*ne lie became two, and two became four – until your life became out

of control, while juggling your lovers with your role as wife and mother.

I love you, My child, but I am a just and holy God.

Romans 1:24-25, 6:23, Psalm 111:7, Isaiah 6:3

*M*y errant child – your choices had led you to a shattered life, home, and marriage. Were you running from Me? You had experienced My love near death when a horse fell on you. Was I not worthy of your love?

Romans 6:23, Psalm 139:7-8, Revelation 4:11

*I*n your pride, you refused to acknowledge that I have given you everything that you had. I took back your health, your home, your marriage, and your children. James 1:17, Job 1:21, Deuteronomy 28:15

$\mathcal{T}$hen, My child, you listened to people who told you the nice things you wanted to hear – people who called evil good and deceived you by turning My truth into lies.   Micah 2:11, Isaiah 5:20, 30:9-10, Ephesians 4:14

$\mathcal{I}$ had allowed people of the darkness into your life, whose allegiance was not to Me, but to the father of all lies. I watched as they used you for their own gain. Like My Son, you knew betrayal.

Psalm 14:4, John 8:44, Mark 14:44-45

*M*y own creation – I was near and watched you in despair. I saw you run here and there, looking for your own truth and not to Me, even though My living water was near. Instead of desiring My Tree of Eternal Life, you lusted after the Tree of Knowledge, choosing your self to be as god – and not Me. Hosea 7:16, John 4:10, Genesis 3:1-7

*Y*ou obeyed the evil serpent in My garden and your disobedience brought death to our relationship. You made sacrifices on strange altars of self, pursued mental addictions, and sought peace and knowledge from stars, crystals, and false spiritual guides. In your service to others, you were using the force of the earth, which is not from Me.

Genesis 3:7-24, Hosea 10:1-2, Deuteronomy 18:9-14, Acts 7:42

$\mathcal{M}$y confused one – you traded Me and your rock of confession in My Son, Jesus, for knowledge and mindless practices. You worshiped what I created, not Me. The gods of other peoples became a snare of death to you, as you sought answers using divination to the dark side.

Matthew 16:13-18, Romans 1:25, Isaiah 8:19-20, 47:8-13, Joshua 23:13

*T*hen you were all alone on your little rock of what you thought to be the truth. The more I called to you, the more you rebelled and polluted yourself with spiritual adultery by pursuing those other gods.

Hosea 11:1-2, Psalm 102:7, Exodus 20:3-6,14, Isaiah 57:7-11

*M*y desolate one – I purposely made your body unable to tolerate alcohol and medication. If you are to be My child of truth, you will have to know truth. This will set you free! You cannot escape from life and reality, as you almost did. I still called you, pursuing you, for I am a jealous God, your Father, Maker, and Husband.

John 8:32, Song of Songs 2:8, Isaiah 54:5

*Y*ou became a shadow of your former self, with several illnesses overcoming you. I called you to change your ways and return to Me. Facing the truth is healing and far better than masking the pain, which makes you ill. Life *can* grow out of the pain you have been through.

Psalm 102:4-7, Deuteronomy 28:15-68, Malachi 3:7, Proverbs 3:7-8

$\mathscr{M}$y little sparrow – I placed a hedge of thorns of fear and depression in your life. Worldly judgment and revenge were tormenting you on every side. I was waiting for you to turn back to Me.

Hosea 2:6, 2 Corinthians 12:7, Acts 2:38

*W*hen your life spiraled downward, you were overwhelmed with depression and despair. You realized the mistakes you had made, the people you had hurt, and that no one could help you – and that you had to face Me! Psalms 50:52, 69:15, 88:6

My child – the time came to release My wrath upon you in judgment. Your life was in shambles and I was going to leave you in darkness. I gave you the freedom to choose – and in your disobedience your choices were evil and selfish.   Romans 2:1-16, Psalm 7:11-12, Lamentations 3:1-14

$\mathcal{B}$ut I saw a tear fall from My Son's face. He had been weeping and praying for you. In My mercy, I allowed you to see it. Your heart realized that it was He whom you sought for forgiveness. How I rejoiced when you turned to Him from being a slave to sin!

Romans 6, 8:34, John 11:35, Psalm 103:13, Acts 3:19, Colossians 1:13-14

His PRESENCE

Ah, I know You! And I've seen You before!
While lying, dying at death's dark door
When I left my broken body in the street –
Your blazing Presence I came to meet.

Oh, the warmth and acceptance from above
Which you gave my thirsty heart in love,
A glorious Presence of light and trust –
Which I grasped as my body lay in the dust.

Now, dear Lord, my poor spirit is broken
But You've shown me the door and have spoken
Words to my heart on the breath of silence
That healed all conflict and inner torments.

Oh, Jesus, I love You – for You've given
Me a life of joy with many sins shriven,
Living within me as well as without –
Now I know what peace and love are about!

Denise Park 1985

SEASON 3
Healing

*A*nd I will reaffirm My covenant with
you, and you will know that I am the
LORD. You will remember your sins and
cover your mouth in silence and shame
when I forgive you of all that you have
done, says the Sovereign LORD. . . for
I am the LORD that healeth thee.

Ezekiel 16:62-63 NLT, Exodus 15:26 KJV

✝

oh my G…o…d – i am so ashamed and c-r-y out to You, begging You to hear me, Your errant child.

i feel like a specter, a waif on the streets of destruction.

i have run far from You and have done much wrong.

i need to feel Your Son's love once again. hear me, Father, for You are the Source of all that i am.

Psalms 50:15, 102:2-6, Acts 2:38

i have come to the end of my rope. i feel that my life has ended.

my sins and bad choices have choked the strength out of me and my will to live. they have robbed me of life.

i am undone. have mercy on me.

give me a sign that You are there and still care, that Your Son, Jesus, who showed me so much love, will help me.

Psalms 22:11-15, 63:1, 140:6,
Lamentations 5:16, Isaiah 6:5

*Y*es, I am Jesus, the Lover of your soul, the Lily of the Valley, who loves you with an everlasting love. I, and the Father, rejoice that you have cried out to Us. We welcome you with a kiss and an embrace!

John 14:11, Song of Songs 2:1, Luke 15:3-7, 11-24

𝒥 came to live on earth to bring you life. I am the way to reconcile you to the Father, the truth spoken about His Word, and the life and light for all people. I am the sacrifice made for your sins. I have ransomed you. Just believe!   John 1:4, 14:6, 16:9, Revelation 5:8-14, Mark 10:45

$\mathcal{M}$y dearly beloved child – your Father wants you to come sit with Us in the garden and talk. You need spring to come into your life, once again, and to find that you have never been far from Our heart. We are your Friends. Genesis 3:1-13, Song of Songs 2:10-12, 8:13, John 15:15

*M*y child – I am always your Father. My Spirit will convict you of your errors, and together We will sculpt you into the beautiful person I created you to be. I see you through My Son, the Lamb, who was the perfect sacrifice for your sins. Now your garments will be white as snow!

Luke 4:18, Hebrews 9:13-15, Revelation 7:13-17

$\mathscr{M}$y dearest child – I gave you a lifeline of faith to hold on to while I waited for you to call out to Me. This you did well, as it was all you had left when dark times came. I am pleased that you held on with what strength you had left.

Matthew 8:10, 17:20

I gave you the gift of hope, when you offered My Son to take charge of your life. When you live in Him, He will live in you. Now you will have this beautiful hope of His glory in your life. Keep your eyes on Him, your Lord, Savior, Friend, and Lover.

Colossians 1:27, Psalm 123:2,
John 15:4-7,14-15, Song of Songs 2:16

$\mathcal{I}$ am the Lord, your Redeemer. Come to the still waters, My child, and I shall heal your wounds and refresh you. In My anger I hid My face from you for a moment, but I will show you that My love and mercy are new every morning. Psalms 23:2, 46:10, Isaiah 54:8, Jeremiah 30:17, Lamentations 3:22-23

$\mathcal{M}$y child – I am a Father who forgives and pities His children. My Son's sacrifice made it possible to bring you back to Me. I will hold you close with feathers of love and comfort you as a mother comforts her child.

Psalms 86:5, 91:4, 103:13, Romans 5:1-11,18, Isaiah 66:13

*S*in separated you far from Me and cut deep into your soul, leaving open

wounds. I punished and rebuked you severely, as a father would – but that

is because I love you. Psalms 15, 32, 90:8, Hebrews 12:5-13, Revelation 3:19

$\mathcal{S}$peak to Me, My child! You cannot hide from Me! I will speak tenderly to you and lead you away from your desert wilderness. I will transform your valley of trouble into a gateway of hope and miracles. Come to Me, for I am a compassionate father.

Psalms 25:6-7, 86:15, 103:13, 139:7-8, Hosea 2:14-15

$\mathcal{M}$y child – open the gates of your heart and I will heal the broken pieces and bandage up those wounds which have been inflicted on you. Your path will be long and hard – but straight to Me, your loving Father. Hosea 6:1, Matthew 7:13-14

$\mathcal{L}$et go of your past and your fears. Use your faith to come to Me. You are a new person in My Son – one created in My likeness. I will be faithful to you and gather you back to Me. You will know me as your holy God and loving Father. Trust Me!

Ephesians 4:20-24, Hosea 2:20,
Psalms 9:10, 37:3

$\mathcal{M}$y child of grace-given – there is no need to be proud or stubborn. You found My sign to you and I rejoiced! I am pleased to see that you are throwing out books, pictures, and crystals that do not glorify Me.

Deuteronomy 9:13, Acts 19:13-20

*D*ear one – open up your wounded heart and give it to Me. I long to care for you. I have found you and chosen you to be mine. My Son brought you back to Me through the cross. I love you. Come!

Psalms 109:21-22, 147:3, Exodus 20:2-6, John 15-16, Mark 10:45

*M*y wounded child – though you are perfect to Me in your spirit through My Son, Jesus, let Me show you what has to be cleansed in yourself and thrown out. I want My Spirit to dwell more fully in you. Sin in your life has left a mess!

1 Corinthians 3:12-17, Romans 7:14-25, Galatians 5:16-22, James 1:21

$\mathscr{A}$s a start, I will gently shear off the pride hiding your pain, uncleanness, involvement with the occult, and generational sin. You will find a new life of awe and freedom knowing Me as your Father. I keep My promises. I call you to be holy before Me or you will not be able to see Me.

Jeremiah 32:17-18, John 14:7, 15:1-2,
Deuteronomy 18:9-14, 27:11-28:68, Hebrews 12:14

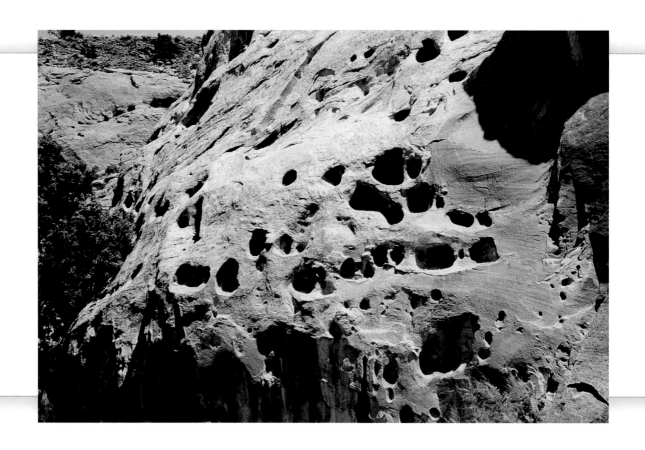

*L*ook, My child – your false beliefs, which you held, fell away and left holes in your mind and spirit. You are feeling weak and powerless as you try to redirect your life. You are being convicted, but I will show you an opened door where My Holy Spirit will meet you. Just ask Him and He will direct you to Me. I am your life. Romans 1:21-23, Matthew 16:25, John 16:8

$\mathcal{S}$atan, who controls this world, and his demons will wage war on you to reclaim you. You, in fact, have defected from the kingdom of darkness to My Kingdom of Light. Quickly fill these holes with My written Word and truth!

Matthew 12:43-45, Ephesians 6:10-18, Psalms 73, 105, 119:2, John 14:6, 1 John 5:19

*M*y precious child – I give you great encouragement as I see that your will demands the demons of darkness to leave – especially those of lust and divination. I will heal your wounds from shame and rejection. Forgive, forgive, forgive! That is when I will see signs of growth in your dry places.

Psalms 30:7, 145:3, Exodus 15:26, Matthew 6:9-15

*A*s you soak in or meditate on My Word, I will lead you to a place of truth and rest in Me. Ask and I will give, knock and doors will be opened to you. Listen to My Son, Jesus, who has the waters of life flowing from Me.

Psalm 143:5-6, Hebrews 4:1,
Matthew 7:7, John 4:14, 14:6

$\mathcal{L}$ook around, My beloved child, and see My grace and love for you through people, provision, and in My creation! Hold on to the words your Father speaks to you. I am here! Psalms 8, 29, 121

$\mathcal{D}$o not dwell on things of the past. I am doing a new work in you.
It will spring forth as I transform you by changing the way you think.
Then you will begin to have the mind of My Son. You will yearn for
My will as you seek the fruitful thing to do.

Isaiah 43:18-19, 1 Corinthians 2:16, Romans 12:2

*M*y broken child – remember that I am your Master Potter and you are the work of My hands. I will take your broken pieces and create something new in you. My light will shine through the cracks of your weakness. Genesis 1:27, Isaiah 43:18-19, 64:8, 2 Corinthians 12:9-10

$\mathcal{L}$ook for teachers and guides along your road to recovery. I have assigned a disabled person and one in prison to encourage you. I want you to see that I choose to work through those whom you think are inferior to you. They are My dear children, too.

Isaiah 30:20-21, 1 John 1:7, Psalm 103:13

$\mathcal{M}$y beloved – where you were broken in life is where resurrection can begin. New life is born out of the blood of pain and sacrifice. I have removed your sins from you – as far as the East is from the West. Look to Me, for I am your tender and compassionate Father.

Romans 12:1, John 12:24,
Psalms 103:12-13, 118:17-18

$\mathcal{G}$uard your faith, My child. I know that you are overwhelmed by worldly pressures and by the consequences of your acts. Rest in Me as I wipe your tears and soothe your frayed nerves with soft flakes of My love and healing.

Hebrews 11:1, Joshua 1:8, Jeremiah 30:17

*D*o not complain, My child, for it is the rough things – and people – which I bring into your life, that build your character and polish you into My beautiful jewel.

1 Corinthians 10:10, Luke 3:4-6,
James 1:2-4, Malachi 3:17

_R_ejoice, My little one! I will take away
your pain and confusion. I will replace
them with the living waters of a full and
prosperous life. As you seek to drink
from the waters of My love which My
Son, Jesus, pours on you, My peace,
which passes all understanding, will
permeate your soul.

1 Corinthians 14:33,
John 7:37-38, 10:10, Philippians 4:7

*M*y child – I am so proud that you are seeking to please Me by releasing the logs, or sins, belonging to others, and are offering up your own to Me. I treasure your pleas asking Me to change you. You will be less burdened. Can you forgive yourself? Luke 6:41-42, 11:4, Proverbs 16:7

$\mathscr{M}$y dearest child – I hold your grateful heart in the palm of My hand
with such joy! I lovingly laugh with the trust you are giving Me, which
honors Me. I want to bless you so much! Psalm 37:3-7, 1 Thessalonians 5:18

$\mathcal{M}$y beautiful bride – with great love and joy I will put a garland of white flowers, like pearls, one by one, around your neck, adorning you as one of beauty in My Kingdom. Can you fathom the love I have for you?

Song of Songs 4:9, 7:10, Isaiah 61:3, Jeremiah 31:3

$\mathcal{Y}$ou will be among other jewels, which you have seen on My robe. They are My precious children who love and serve Me with singleness of heart.

Malachi 3:17, Isaiah 6:1,
Colossians 3:22-23

WHERE HAVE THEY TAKEN *My* LORD

Shivering in the dark without a word,
Feeling my soul rent as if by a sword,
I cry to touch His body in the tomb
Which gave me such joy like a babe in the womb –
    Where have they taken my Lord?

I am exhausted from suffering agony and pain
Of seeing Him hanging on a cross, a king to reign
But instead crucified as a common thief
Or for something else far beyond my belief –
    Where have they taken my Lord?

Oh, the ignominy and bitter shame
That the Son of God should bear in our name,
Yet there He hung proudly without a sigh,
An embodiment of love, which we all deny –
    Where have they taken my Lord?

My heart feels so empty and cold
And opened to dark horrors untold –
Where is the Love that heals the pain,
The Light that shows the way to live again?
    Where have they taken my Lord?

Denise Park 1985

SEASON 4
Knowing God

*F*or the Father Himself loves you dearly

because you love Me (Jesus) and believe

that I came from God.   John 16:27 NLT

✝

I AM that I AM. I am the Ancient of Days, the high and lofty One who inhabits eternity! I am the Supreme Being, the Mighty Warrior God of Israel, the Father of all that I have created. I am the Creator of you and the universe. My throne is in the heavens; the earth is My footstool.

Exodus 3:14, 15:3, Daniel 7:9, Genesis 1, Isaiah 1:24, 57:15, 66:1, Malachi 2:10

There is no other God beside Me but I manifest in three Persons: I am the Father – then in My Son, Jesus, who came to earth, and in My Spirit. You, My child, are one of many whom I have created in My image – soul, body, and spirit. I long for you to know Me.

Isaiah 45:21, John 17, 16:7, Genesis 1:27, 1 Thessalonians 5:23

*M*y lovely child – I longed for a family to be with as you long for your children. I chose a people to lead out of slavery from Egypt, through a sea, and into a desert to know Me. As a Father, I actually fed them and cared for them for forty years – but they preferred to return as slaves to their bondage instead of being in My holy Presence.

Exodus 12:31, 14:15-15:26, 16:3-17, Deuteronomy 29:2-6

_D_uring the day, I went before them in a pillar of cloud, and at night, a pillar of fire. I showed them My glory, covering their tent of worship, and filling it with My Presence. Yet they complained and rebelled against Me. In My wrath, I let only two of those, whom I had freed, come into the Promised Land, which I had prepared for them.

Exodus 13:21, 40:34, Deuteronomy 1:26-39

$\mathcal{T}$hey came into My Promised Land with the children of those whom
I had led across the desert for forty years – longer than necessary, but
they were not able to be taught. They grew into a great number of people
occupying the land, and they prospered.

Joshua 1 & 3, Psalm 105:24, 2 Chronicles 14:7

*B*ut My child, in their prosperity they became fat, proud, and complacent – thinking that they no longer needed Me. They turned from Me to other idols and gods, forgetting Me – the One who fathered them and gave them birth. Deuteronomy 32:15-18, Hosea 13:4-6

I had called together a people to become a holy nation, a kingdom of priests to be ruled by Me. But they forsook Me. I burned with anger and wanted to destroy them. I taunted this people to call on their kings and their gods for help. I wanted to bring forth death, terrors, and illness! Exodus 19:5-6, 2 Kings 17:7-18, Hosea 13:4-16

$\mathcal{B}$ut I am God, and not man. My heart is torn within Me. My compassion and mercy overflow. My people cannot keep My covenant. Repeatedly they turn away from Me. I, then, let their enemies turn them back to Me. When I hear their cries, I will bless them once again and be their God. Hosea 11:8-11, 2 Kings 17:7-16, Psalm 62:12, The Old Testament

I am a most holy and just God. I cannot live with darkness and sin.
How can I gather My people – and others who are bound to Me
through their belief – into My presence when sin separates us? I want
to protect them and sing songs of love to them.

Romans 11, Hosea 11:9, Psalm 9:7-10, Song of Songs

My beloved – remember your Creator, for I alone stretched out the heavens and by Myself I made the earth and everything in it. I own all things, including you and the cattle on a thousand hills.

Ecclesiastes 12:1, Job 38-41, Genesis 1:1,27, Psalm 50:10

$\mathcal{L}$isten, My little one: I look down from heaven on all mankind to see if there is anyone one who desires My Presence – for just one who would seek to understand My revelations which I would share in our intimate quiet times.

Psalm 53:2, Daniel 2:28

I will rescue those who love Me. I will protect those who trust Me, shielding them with My wings and sheltering them with My feathers. I will answer when they call and satisfy them with a long life. I will show them My glory, for I am their inheritance and their cup of blessing.

Psalms 16:5, 91:4,14-16

I am not like any other God! I want My people to know Me as *their* God, and for them to seek Me with their whole hearts, minds, and souls. I want them to come deeper and deeper into Me in search of truth and to experience My unending love for them as a husband has for his wife.

Psalm 86:8, Matthew 22:37, Isaiah 44:6, 54:4-8

$\mathcal{L}$ike you, My child, I want My people to know My heart. I will replace their hearts of stone with new hearts of flesh. Then they will want to become one with My heart. King David, who wrote many of the psalms, was a man after My own heart. Ezekiel 36:26, Jeremiah 24:7, 1 Samuel 13:14

*L*ook, My child! I have made a new covenant with My people. I now write My laws on their hearts and in their minds. My laws simply guard and build our relationship and yours with others. Now all will know Me as their God and that they are My people. Jeremiah 31:33-34, Hebrews 8:9-12

I will forgive their evil ways and wash away their sin and be as a caring father to them. I will remove their rebellious acts from them – as far away as the East is from the West.

Jeremiah 3:19, 31:34, 1 Peter 5:7, Psalms 51:7, 68:4-5, 103:12

*M*y beloved child – believe My promises! My rainbow in the heavens

is a sign that I am faithful to My Word of this new and better covenant.

Genesis 9:13, 2 Timothy 3:16-17

*M*y old covenant of the law, which My people had agreed to obey, became impossible for them to do so. Now they will be redeemed by what I have done. They will return to Me singing and will be overcome with happiness! Hebrews 8, Isaiah 51:11

I sit on My throne and closely watch the goings and comings of My people. I, and the four beasts around Me with many eyes, will testify of this new thing I have done in the history of the world, which I call My people to see. Psalms 11:4, 99:1-5, Isaiah 43:19, Revelation 4:6-9

*M*y curious child – who has known My mind, the depth of My wisdom, My unsearchable ways, and judgments? Just as the heavens are higher than the earth, so are My ways and thoughts higher than yours.

Romans 11:33-34, 1 Corinthians 2:16, Isaiah 55:9

*R*ead, My child, how I have come to earth to visit My people in a form similar to them. There was Adam, Abraham, Jacob, Joshua, Gideon, and others who saw Me and worshiped Me.

Genesis 3:8, 18:1-33, 32:24-30,
Joshua 5:13-15, Judges 6:11-24

The new thing is that I chose to come to earth, Myself, through a woman to live among you. I have missed walking with My people. I longed to reconcile them to Me. Because of My love, I wanted to make this sacrifice that would fulfill the legal requirement for sin by law, for all time, and to sign this new covenant with My own blood – as a man.

2 Corinthians 5:17-21, Matthew 5:17, John 19:30, Hebrews 9:1-28

I found a beautiful, pure woman, Mary, who loved and trusted Me to the point of going against her culture and enduring shame to obey Me. She rejoiced and praised My name! Her betrothed husband questioned her pregnancy, but I spoke to him. Luke 1:26-38,46-55, Matthew 1:18-25

I was humbly born in a stable in Bethlehem, as was prophesied. Angels, shepherds, and foreign wise men came to worship Me, but the rulers of My country tried to kill Me.   Micah 5:2, Luke 2:1-20, Matthew 2:1-12,16-18

A prophet called Me "Immanuel," which means "God with you," but My angel, Gabriel, asked Mary to call Me "Jesus," meaning "Salvation of God." I grew up among you, learning obedience to My Father as a man. I showed you how to be obedient, how to resist temptation to sin, and how to stay connected with Me in heaven.

Isaiah 7:14, Luke 1:31, 2:51-52, Hebrews 5:2,8, 4:15

I taught about My Kingdom in heaven coming to earth. The good news
is that I came to call you to return to Me and I will forgive your sins.
I healed those who called on Me. I poured out My love and living waters
on mankind – and My blood.

Matthew 4:17, Luke 4:40, 24:47, John 4:10, 19:34

*L*isten, My child! There were many sheep who heard My voice. I loved being with My people! I shepherded them into a full life, showing them My love as both their Friend and "Abba" Father. My Son rightly declared that if you had seen Him, you had seen Me.

John 10:1-18,30, 14:9, 15:15, Mark 14:36, 2 Peter 1:1, 2 Corinthians 4:4

*Y*et I allowed the evil darkness to direct My life for a moment. The self-righteous religious leaders were jealous and angry. My friends betrayed Me, denied Me, and most all – just left. It was time to seal and enact My new covenant between mankind and Me.   Luke 22:1-6,53-62

Oh, My child — I came to earth to do a glorious thing, but My people arrested Me, spat on Me, falsely tried Me, beat and whipped Me, and called for My death. I was hung and crucified on a cross between two criminals. But in My great love for My people, which you could never begin to understand, I paid for their sins and bore their sicknesses for all time. I had paid the price and fulfilled all prophesies.

Luke 22:47-23:49, Isaiah 52:13-53:12

The earth blackened and shook. My body was taken off the cross and friends properly prepared Me for burial in a tomb nearby. But a grave couldn't keep Me! I rose on the third day and appeared to Mary Magdalene first, then to My disciples, showing them My wounds as proof. I ate, taught, and enjoyed them for forty days. I left them with hope and a promise that I would return.

Matthew 27:45-66, Luke 24, Acts 1:2-11

$\mathcal{I}$, the Father, keep My promises. My Son was reunited with Me in heaven. True to My covenant word, I chose to send Our Spirit in power – not to live in a building, but to live in the hearts of man – Our home with Our people on earth. John 16:5-11, Acts 1:4-8, 2:1-21, Hebrews 8

$\mathcal{M}$y old covenant with My people was a shadow and a promise of things to come. The new brings fulfillment and the realization of your inheritance with Me as your Father. My Son has done all of this for you!

Hebrews 8 and 9

*M*y Son's death tore away any barrier between you and Me. The life-giving waters of My Spirit will be able to rush down from My throne to My people, who seek Me through Him. There are many deceiving spirits around who avoid My Son – but only one Holy Spirit from Us.

Hebrews 10:19-20, Revelation 7:17,
Acts 2:38, 1 John 4:1-6

*O*nly Our Spirit can change the hearts of people. Only through Him can the peace of My Kingdom be brought to earth and unify My people. He is My gift to you. Seek His guidance and counsel. Ask Him and He will reveal Me and My Son, Jesus, to you – and the mysteries and desires of Our heart.

Acts 2, Jeremiah 33:3, John 16:5-15

*M*y precious one – let My written Words speak and grow in your spirit. They will reveal truth to you – not the world's, but Mine. I have made you and I know what is best for you. My laws are perfect and give life, not death. They are simple – line upon line, precept upon precept, to instruct you in the way you should live.

2 Timothy 3:16, Isaiah 28:13, Psalm 32:8

*D*ear one – don't let anyone keep you from reading My Word. It is fire and a hammer that smashes rocks into pieces. It is what I have spoken to My people who know Me. Your life will expand and bloom after being in a cold, rigid mold. I yearn for you to begin to know Me, as I know you.

Jeremiah 23:29, John 1:1-5, 5:39, 16:12-15, Revelation 1:3, 22:6-7,17

*M*y precious pearl – My Word is a love letter to you. Prepare a straight way to Me. You did not receive much nurture as a child, but I will come to you and feed you like a father and carry you in My arms against My heart. You *are* My pearl of great price!   Isaiah 40:1-13, Matthew 13:45-46

*T*hings of the world may last for a season, but I AM and My Word is forever. My Son, Jesus, is the Word! Through Him you will discover eternal life. You also will experience My mercy and unending love – which I have just for you! 2 Corinthians 4:18, John 1:1-5, 5:39, Romans 6:23, Psalm 106:1

*I*n Me, My child, your life will become a promise of miracles and sacrifice, of heaven and suffering, not in the world, but in Me. All of these seeds of promise, as in My Word, will lead you on your path of salvation and sanctification.

Luke 8:11-15, Psalms 77:14, 105:4-5, Philippians 2:12, Hebrews 2:10

*C*ome, My beloved, on this road of salvation, for it leads to My holiness toward bringing the glory of My Kingdom into the world. My Kingdom is in you. When you look for it and make this your priority, you will have My power and provisions. This is My government and I am the King. Seek Kingdom living! Psalm 145:11-13, Matthew 6:10-13,33, 1 Corinthians 4:20

$\mathcal{S}$o, dearest child of My heart – open your heart, even your mouth, and
I will fill it with a new song and good things. I will rejoice over you
and sing a happy song to you. Psalms 40:3, 81:10, Zephaniah 3:17

I say, rise up My beloved, My beautiful one, and come away with Me. Your

winter is past, the flowers are springing up, and the birds are singing.

I will cover you with My wings and tell you how much I love you!

Song of Songs 2:10-12, Psalm 91:4

ECSTASY

Look at the little nest I have found
Upon the shining moss covering the ground.
Come, my Spouse, come here and lay with me –
Lay with me in the rhythm of ecstasy!

Listen, my Love – there is ne'er a sound
In this hideaway nest I have found
For the birds are at watch in the tree
And the animals wait for what is to be.

What ecstasy and joy! The bells are ringing!
The cymbals clash in glorious thanksgiving!
For there is no one else to share this with me
But you, my Love, in this nest beneath the tree.   Denise Park 1983

SEASON 5
Marriage

Y ou are like a private garden, my treasure, my bride! You are like a spring that no one else can drink from, a fountain of my own.

Song of Songs 4:12 NLT

*M*y beloved – I have heard your prayer for sending someone to be a reason for you to come out of your prison of depression, to understand you, to help you with your legal work – and just to care.

Luke 11:5-13, Proverbs 17:17

$\mathcal{E}$ven though you may not want a mate, I have one for you as a gift from
Me, your Father, who knows your needs before you do – and tends
to them. Matthew 6:8, Song of Songs 5:16

My child – leave your negative thoughts, worries, and fears behind. I am your loving Father and encourage you to be tenderhearted, forgiving, forbearing, and kind to one another. 1 John 4:15-21, Psalm 18:28, Ephesians 4:32

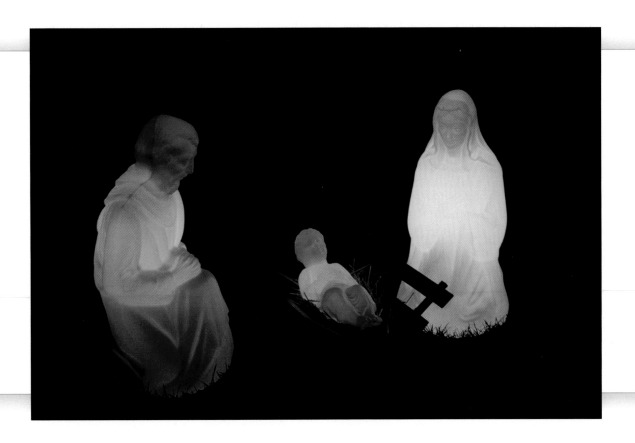

*Y*es, My children – know that when you keep your eyes on Me, then your relational problems will be few. Your love will grow for each other as you see the other through Me – forgiven and precious!

1 Corinthians 13:4-7, Ephesians 5:1-2

*L*ook, dear ones – I found both of you empty and hollow from worldly pleasures and wounds. You no longer can stand alone without Me. Let Me fill you. I am *Jehovah Rophe*, the LORD who heals you.

Psalm 103:1-5, Romans 15:13, Exodus 15:26

I want you as beautiful olive trees in My garden – not ones being heavy with burdens of anger, fear, and shame. These burdens would multiply and prey on each other. Be rooted and grounded in My love and you will have My blessing.

Psalm 52:8, Ephesians 3:17, 4:17-28

When you make a covenant of marriage before Me, I have to be in the middle of your relationship – or it will be a battle of control and failed expectations. Honor Me and I will give you a supernatural love for the other.   Proverbs 21:19, Ephesians 4:29-32, 5:21-30, Psalm 20:7-8

My children – let your mouths bless each other and not speak words that curse, cut, or wound. Guard and discipline your tongue, for it can bring life or death. James 3

At the end of each day, before the sun goes down, My dear ones, search the pools of your hearts for any residue of anger. This could be a door for the devil to come in and plant resentment and bitterness in you. Confess to Me and to each other. Ephesians 4:26-27, Hebrews 12:15, 1 John 1:6-9

*L*ike the beauty of these leaves, which fall to the ground in death, let go of any past grievances of anger and unforgiveness toward others – or they will be a part of your relationship. I want the two of you together in My Kingdom – cleansed and clothed with My righteousness, peace, and joy in My Spirit. Whatever you do will be known to Me.

Matthew 6:14, 11:30, John 12:24, Psalm 11:4, Galatians 5:16-23

$\mathcal{R}$ejoice! I am a living God who keeps the promises I made in My Word and who showers you with many blessings! I will make all things possible for you. Look for Me, call to Me, cling to Me!

1 Peter 1:4, Ephesians 1:3,
Mark 9:23, Acts 11:23

*Y*our marriage will be an exciting work of how you are becoming alive in Me. I am renewing your lives from the past. Marriage on earth is a reflection of how My people will be with Me in My Kingdom in heaven.

Joel 2:25, John 3:27-29, Matthew 2:2

$\mathcal{M}$y beloved children – hold each other close as one. Be oh, so tender with each other! Both of you are Mine, whom I shelter in the world. Together, as one, you can stand through the difficulties you will have in life. Ephesians 4:32, Psalm 91:1, John 16:33

*D*elight in each other, for I have sent My Son to give you life more abundantly! He makes the best wine at weddings. Celebrate – for you are My gift to each other! And don't forget to dance with Me.

Song of Songs 4:9, John 2:1-11, 10:10

*M*y dear ones – invite Me to live in your home. Honor Me and I will give you a safe haven. I am a mighty God, your fortress in a world which is at enmity with Me.

Joshua 24:14-15, Psalm 18:2, James 4:4

*H*ear My voice calling to you. Come near to Me and I will come near to you. I am your Shepherd who leads you to green pastures, for I am a father who loves to give good things daily to His children.

John 10:3,11, James 1:17, 4:8,
Psalms 23:2, 68:19

$\mathcal{Y}$es, come to Me my beloved children – the two of you as one before Me. I call you to live and love in Me. I joyfully feel your thirst to know Me. My ears delight in hearing you pray together as you seek Me with all your heart, mind, and soul.

Psalms 42:1-2, 107:8-9, Matthew 22:37, Acts 17:28, Isaiah 55:6

*D*rink, My children. I am the living water. As in the story about the sower and the seed – My water goes over or around the rocks, through the sand, but rests in good soil. There it will nourish those roots which seek to drink and be refreshed.

John 4:10, 14, Matthew 13:3-9,18-23

There is a highway to holiness on your journey. My prophet, John, told you to turn from your sins to Me, your God, and to make your path straight for My coming. He pleaded for you to fill in the valleys of wrong choices and to level the mountains of idols and acquisitions. My children – if I am to meet you halfway from My holy mountain, I don't want to stub My toe when I walk with you!

Luke 3:3-16, Isaiah 2:3, 35:8, 40:3-5

$\mathcal{L}$ook, My children – the trees, which you have tried to climb in your past, have fallen, as have your tears. All is dead wood now. But there are cones which have released their seeds. I will redeem your past – for I waste nothing!

Psalm 119:73-75, Isaiah 48:6-9, 52:9, Lamentations 3:58

*Y*es, I am doing a new thing in your lives. Your sadness will be turned into joy. Look forward to being with Me as My beloved son and daughter. Let Me remold and renew your lives. Listen to My voice in your ears as I direct your path. Isaiah 42:9, 30:20-21, Psalms 16:11, 30:11, 1 John 3:1

*D*o not let any evil darkness threaten to crush you. Call Me in the day

of trouble. I will deliver you and you shall glorify Me. My Son came to

be a light to all who believe in Him. Psalms 40:17, 50:15, John 12:46, 1:4-5

$\mathcal{M}$y beloved children – come up higher. I am your towering rock of safety, your secure place where your enemies cannot reach you. I will reveal more of My mysteries to you as you live in and digest My Word.

Psalm 61:2-3, Hebrews 5:11-14, Luke 8:10

$\mathcal{C}$ome, drink from Me, the fountain of life, which you both share together. Encourage and nurture each other from My well. The world can be a tempting and difficult place, and the flesh can be trying – but I am here to restore and refresh you.

Revelation 21:6, 1 John 2:15-16, Psalm 23:3

*M*y turtledoves – your winter is past and it is time for singing! Enjoy the gift of your home with which I have blessed you. You have a special love and devotion to share with only the other. You are one before Me. Honor each other in this way.

Song of Songs 2:10-11, 4:12-15, Proverbs 5:15-19, Matthew 19:4-6

$\mathscr{L}$ook at these little wild flowers along your path called "Bloodroots." They will remind you that your cleansing and purification does come from your being rooted and grounded in My Son. He is the One who gave you a blood covering for your redemption and protection.

Hebrews 13:11-12, Colossians 2:6-7, Ephesians 3:17, Psalm 51:7

$\mathcal{M}$y children – this represents the "pot of gold" with which I have blessed you. Honor Me with your wealth, trusting that I will fill all your needs. Talk to Me about them. When I am your banker, you will have far less stress!

Philippians 4:19, 1 Timothy 6:10, Proverbs 3:9-10

*M*y dear ones – you are the crown of My delight! Take precious moments to let go of the cares of the world – the "Martha" in you, and sit quietly at My feet, listening like Mary. Let us delight in each other! The lilies of the field are beautiful – just gazing at Me.

Luke 10:38-42, Matthew 6:25-34, Psalm 37:4

$\mathcal{Y}$es, I tenderly call you to spend quiet time with Me in My living Word – your Bible. I am the Author who speaks to you! Pray with each other for My Holy Spirit to lead you to greater understanding. Try others' teachings against My Word so that you will not be deceived.

1 Peter 2:2, 2 Peter 1:20-21,
2 Timothy 3:16, Acts 17:11

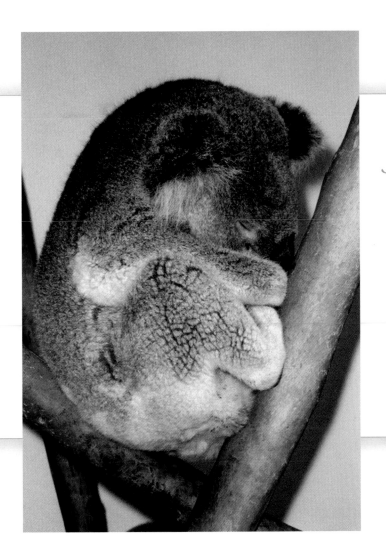

I am the Father who gives rest to His loved ones. I call you to care for your bodies. They are My handiwork. I have bought you for a price and I ask you to honor that. My Spirit is glad to give you health counsel and wisdom – especially since He lives in you. Ask Him!

1 Corinthians 3:16-17, 6:19-20, Psalm 127:2

*N*ot too much rest, My precious ones, for I have a purpose for your life.
I call you to minister to others where I have comforted you. Your servants'
hearts honor Me, serving and encouraging those in need, those in prison,
and widows. You can be a missionary in your own workplace or community!

2 Timothy 1:9, 2 Corinthians 1:3-4, Matthew 25:31-46, James 1:27

I have prepared a house of prayer for you where you will be filled with joy being a part of the Body of My Son, Jesus. It is important to be among those who love Me and seek the truth in My Word. Bring your share of My light and the power of My Spirit to bless others and your community.

Isaiah 56:7, 1 Corinthians 12, 2 Corinthians 6:14, 2 Timothy 2:15

$\mathcal{T}$o rest in Me, My children, means that you will have My peace after labor. In turn, you are called to go and bear fruit. You have been grafted into My family through My Son, the true vine, to live and bear fruit from the gifts which I have given you – in order for Me to bless others through you.

Hebrews 4:10-11, John 15:1-17

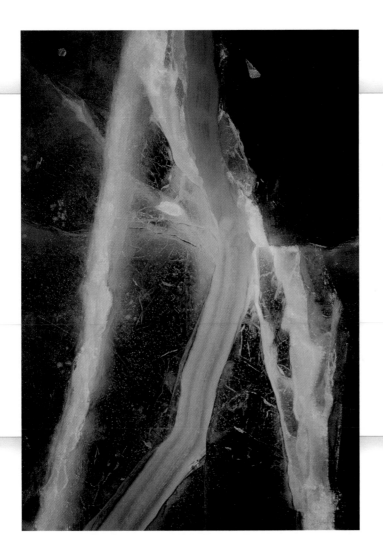

*N*o ministry or miracles are done in My name without the power of My Spirit. Even My Son needed Me to give Him the Holy Spirit before He started His ministry on earth. The power of My Spirit can shake the earth and through My Son, Jesus, can bring My people together as one.

Mark 16:15-18, Luke 3:21-22,
Acts 1:8, 4:31, John 17:20-23

*M*y children – I create families for support, nurture, and protection. Since you have had your natural families, I will place others, who love Me, in your lives to be your family. Matthew 12:48-50, 1 John 3:16-17

$\mathcal{Y}$ou are not alone. My children are your real family. Be gentle and love them. Pray together. Live like an orchestra. Play your instrument, gift, or calling with Me as your Conductor.

Hebrews 2:11, 10:25, Acts 12:12, 1 Corinthians 12:13-14, 26-27

*I*t is time for you to gather people around you to speak to them about Me. Feed them at My table during the dark uncertain days ahead. It is through you that I can begin to be a parent to some of My little ones.

2 Timothy 4:2-5, 3:1-4, Romans 8:14-17

*L*et My light shine through you in this dark world. Dear ones, comfort My people. They are thirsty. Feed My lambs. Love each other and be united in Me. Divided, you are left open to the winds of evil in the world.

Matthew 5:14-16, John 21:15, Isaiah 40:1, 55:1-6, Luke 11:17-23

$\mathcal{D}$ear children – as you work in the world for My Kingdom, I am calling you to be perfected and mature in the Body of My Son, the Church. I long for a Bride with a pure, passionate heart for Him, wearing garments of belief.

Ephesians 4:11-16, Colossians 1:18, Song of Songs 3, Matthew 22:1-14, 25:1-13

$\mathcal{I}$ am Jesus, your Bridegroom, who calls you to know My lover's touch. You will be led step by step as you draw near to Me, walking in faith and seeking Me with your whole heart. I have prepared a beautiful room in My Father's house for you when we meet. Can you bear the width and depth of the love I have for you?

Psalm 37:23, Song of Songs 1:4, John 14:1-3, 16:27, Ephesians 3:18-19

*M*y beloveds – I want you to always walk in our Father's Presence. When Our Holy Spirit convicts you of the least sin, when you lean to the ways of the world or to the flesh – confess it immediately! Then you will not be separated from Us and the flow of Our Spirit will not be stifled in you.

John 16:7-9, 1 John 1:9,
Psalm 66:18, 1 Thessalonians 5:19

I want you spotless and purified for My Bride. You are – if you wear My righteousness as your bridal veil. Your lives were difficult when you went through our Father's refining fires, but be filled with Our joy as you come to Me! I am the Lover of your souls, your Bridegroom!

Isaiah 48:10, Song of Songs 4, Revelation 22:17

*M*y victorious ones – I have overcome the world. Your tests and trials have been like a boot camp to prepare you to stand with Me now and when I call you home. I will bless you with a crown of life for your faithfulness and endurance, which I have promised to those who love Me. Then you will see My glory when you enter My heavenly city.

James 1:12, Psalms 103:2-5, 149:4, Revelation 21:1-5, 2 Timothy 4:7-8

$\mathcal{L}$ook, My lovely Bride! Rejoice! The aisle to Me, the sacrificed Lamb, is lined by the trees of My wisdom on a straight path. Let My light shine on your way as you prepare to come to My holy city. I, Jesus, am both with you now – and will greet you when you return.

Isaiah 11:1-3, 35:10, Revelation 5:12, John 1:4-5, Genesis 28:15

$\mathcal{M}$y precious children – you will see Me, your Father, high and lifted up on My throne with My train filling the temple. I stand in My holiness, calling you to come near to Me. My glory in heaven gives it light and My Son, Jesus, who is sitting at My right hand, is its radiant lamp.

Isaiah 6:1, Psalms 46:1-7, 48:1-2, 49:15, Revelation 21:22-24

*Y*ou will see My holy city, the heavenly Jerusalem, with streets of pure gold. You, who are victorious overcomers, will inherit all My blessings. I, as your loving Father, will wipe away all of your tears and pain. As your God, you will see Me in My holiness and majesty.

Revelation 2:7,11,17,26, 3:5,12,21, 21:1-21, Psalms 29:2, 145:5

My INNER CASTLE

At last I have found my reason for living
And feel that I am strong and giving, giving.
To my dear Father, I lift my arms and pray
That I can give some of His love each day.

I come from finding this glow of love within –
A rosy fortress far from the wages of sin,
A castle built on the ashes of identity,
A gossamer-lined nest of serenity.

No longer will I let my past control me
But stand with my Father in eternity
Fighting the devil's schemes and shades of night,
Letting the world bathe in the glory of His light.   Denise Park 1983

SEASON 6
A Call to Prayer

*T*he effectual fervent prayer of a righteous man availeth much. James 5:16 KJV

$\mathcal{M}$ y dearest children – how I am comforted and pleased when I hear your thanksgivings and praise coming up to your almighty Father's ears! Come into the gates of My Kingdom with praise and into My courts before Me with thanksgiving. I live in the praises of My people and will not give My glory to another! Psalms 22:3, 100, Isaiah 48:11

*I*t gives Me great joy to watch you seek answers to the mysteries in My Word. You hear My invitation to know Me. I have set you apart from the world for you to set your eyes upon Me and My Son, Jesus.

Luke 8:10, Revelation 19:9, 1 Peter 2:9-11, Psalm 123:1-2

*C*ome up even higher, My dear ones. It may cost you, but I am calling you to draw close to Me. I call you My friends, as well as My children. I want to show you your inheritance and a new hope in Me.

Psalms 61:2, 73:28, Luke 14:26-35, John 12:32, 15:7,14-15, Lamentations 3:24

*F*rom My throne in heaven, I continually look for any righteous people who will pray to Me on behalf of their families, churches, communities, country, and even for the other nations of the earth – who will perish if they do not serve Me. I need you to care as I do.

Psalm 53:2, 1 Timothy 2:1-3, Isaiah 60:12, Ezekiel 22:30

*C*ome, My people – you are being destroyed when you have no desire to know Me. I call you in love and you do not hear. Because I love you, I sent My only Son to live among you as a light in the darkness, as a Savior to reconcile you to Me. Instead, you rebel against Me and reject Me with your unbelief! Are you against My Son – or for Him?

Hosea 4:6, John 1:5,10-14, 3:16, Colossians 1:19-22, Hebrews 3:12

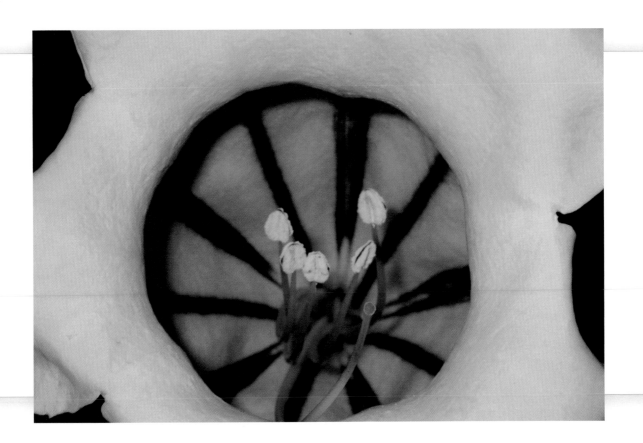

*O*h, My children — I want to draw you close to Me so you will begin to know My heart. You will know My pain as well as My joy. You are a great comfort to Me. I am grieving over My people. They all want a savior from their troubles — but they do not want Me to guide their lives as a loving Father.   John 12:32, Psalm 78:40, Matthew 16:24-26, Romans 14:8-9

$\mathcal{M}$y beloved children – I am guarding you as some of My most precious possessions! I am calling you to Me to become a people who carry My Presence with purpose. Keep your eyes on My Son, the author and finisher of your faith as you come before Me.

Deuteronomy 32:10, Matthew 19:5-6, Hebrews 12:2

*L*ike soldiers for Me, I am calling you to enlist in My army to war – to regain what the enemy has stolen. I will gather others around you who know Me. I will show you the pieces of armor, which My Son has for you: His helmet of salvation, His breastplate of righteousness, His belt of truth, His shoes of peace, His shield of faith, and My Word as a sword. Keep these in place on you and Him with you! Wear Him!

Psalm 108:12-13, Ephesians 6:10-18, John 15:10, Romans 13:14

*Y*es, prayer can be war. I declared war on Satan after he deceived Adam and Eve. My Son won the war. He is your door to victory and release from My curses! I call you to be strong in Me, for the devil will not like you and will seek to devour you. The world is his kingdom. Be not deceived by him through man.

Genesis 3:14-24, Ephesians 6:10-12, 4:14, 1 Peter 5:8, John 14:30, Revelation 20:1-3

*M*y children – be joyful when troubles and persecution come your way, for you need to be rich in character as you grow and mature in the knowledge and love of My Son. Without character and maturity, My gifts can be polluted by your selfish motives. Remember that there is pleasure and the fullness of joy in My Presence!

James 1:2-4, Matthew 5:11-12, 2 Peter 1:3-11, Psalm 16:11

*S*ee these papers stuck in the ruins of the Western Wall of the Temple Mount in Jerusalem? They are prayers from My people all over the world. Like them, I am calling you to pray fervently – for your prayers are heard. They give My Son the joy of sharing Himself with My people, as well as freeing and healing them. Prayers are like letters to and from My throne in heaven.

James 5:16, Luke 4:18,
1 John 5:14-15, Revelation 8:3-4

*M*y dearest ones – ask and pray in the name of My Son, Jesus. I will do what you ask and He will glorify Me. Pray for My treasures who are lost in darkness, and who let the frets and cares of the world choke them. They need to know Me, and the life I have to give them.

John 3:16, 14:13, Isaiah 45:3,
Ezekiel 34:15-16, Mark 4:18-19

I gave My people a white garment of righteousness when My Son died for them. Now they are backslidden and flaunt their sins before Me as this garment becomes tattered and torn. They burden and weary Me with their wickedness. I need you as a witness to My people. You know My Son. Tell others about Him – how much you love Him and how much you know of His love for you.

Jeremiah 3:14-15, Psalm 95:10, Isaiah 43:24, Revelation 12:7-11

$\mathcal{O}$h, that My children would come to Me to loosen their grave cloths, their heavy burdens, and their chains of bondage to sin. One sin leads to another – then all too soon they find themselves enclosed in a cold tomb or in an unfamiliar land, far away from their home in Me.

John 11:38-44, Psalm 55:22, Romans 8:11-21, Luke 15:11-32

$\mathcal{M}$y beloveds – I see you on your knees weeping before Me in worship and pleading for others, like My Son has done for you. Love bears many burdens. You are receiving My heart of love for the people who are sick, oppressed, in pain, or are so lost and far from Me. You are also allowing Me to captivate your heart.

Joel 2:17-18, Galatians 6:2, Hebrews 7:25, Song of Songs 8:10-14

$\mathcal{Y}$our prayers are reaching My ears. My children – your prayers give Me such pleasure, for I am a father who loves to answer His children's requests. When you know My heart, you will know exactly for what and how to pray.   1 Peter 3:12, Revelation 8:3-4, Luke 11:1-13

My blessed ones – I have let you touch My throne. I see your awe and your fear to come any closer. You humbly realize that you cannot possibly attempt to do anything without My grace and help. But you are on My throne – as a partner reigning with My Son at My right hand.

Hebrews 4:14-16, Psalms 24:3-4, 63:2, Philippians 4:13, Revelation 3:20-21, 5:10

You have the gift of faith to take that leap into My Kingdom. Here you will be living in My Presence as you walk in the world with My light. As you lean on Me, I will guide your steps by My Word, and your ears will hear a voice behind you, telling you which way you should go.

1 Corinthians 12:1-9, Psalms 32:8, 119:133, Matthew 5:13-16, Isaiah 30:21

$\mathcal{M}$y children – I call you to ask My Spirit what to pray for and then use your prayer language to speak to Me. My Spirit will come to you and tell you all about My Son and Me – what is on Our heart and in Our will. Many do not receive because they do not ask.

Romans 8:22-27, 1 Corinthians 14:2, John 15:26, James 4:2-3

*L*ook, dear ones – the fields are white for the harvest of souls. There are those who planted seed and those who watered with My Word. I am rejoicing – but now I need more laborers to bring people before My Son, Jesus, with faith, repentance, and belief.

Matthew 13:3,23, Luke 10:2, John 3:5, 16-17, Romans 10:9

*B*e still, My children! Emotional and mental distractions will not allow you to hear My voice deep down inside your spirit. Wait on Me – for My Spirit of wisdom and understanding, counsel and might, knowledge and fear of Me. You will then know your marching orders to carry out.

1 Samuel 12:7, Psalms 27:14, 119:133, Jeremiah 31:33-34, Isaiah 11:2-5

I have gifted you with being watchmen who pass on encouragement to My people. These messages have to be spoken in love. Listen to My wisdom and counsel. Be watchful and faithful in prayer. You will not grow weary if you wait on Me, but will be carried on My wings and filled with My power and strength.

Exodus 14:14, Ezekiel 3:17,
1 Corinthians 13:1-2, Isaiah 40:28-31, 62:6

*M*y Spirit is moving across the earth, searching for more watchmen intercessors to stand and help Me push back this wall of approaching darkness. In Me you are strong enough to do this. Stand, My dear ones, stand with others and pray! Only then can My Spirit and My hosts of angels minister to My people and lessen My judgment.

Psalm 82, Ezekiel 22:30, Hebrews 1:6-7, Ephesians 6:10-18

*D*o My people not see that sin pollutes the land? I need you to pray mightily that your nation will humble itself, repent, and turn back to Me as their God. Then you will see My glory spread out across the land. I do not want to turn My face away from you. There is joy in a nation where I am their Lord! Jeremiah 3:1-9, 2 Chronicles 7:14, Joel 2:13, Psalms 13, 67, 33:12

*P*ray for My people. Then, in My mercy I will sprinkle salt over your nation to stop this stench and leavening of sin. Spiritual adultery of witchcraft and sorcery is rampant. Driving toward reproducing human life is like the people who built the Tower of Babel. I am the Creator of life and they cannot imitate Me! As a Father, I love My people – but I have to discipline them.

1 Corinthians 5:6-8, Deuteronomy 18:10-13, Genesis 11:1-9, Hebrews 12:5-13

My children – bear with Me in grief that My people are no better than the pagans in times past, who threw their babies into the fire to appease their gods. How can they destroy that which I have created in the very image of Myself? How can they decide between life and death for others – for their "god" of convenience? How I weep over this murderous sin!

2 Kings 23:10,13, Leviticus 18:21, Genesis 1:27, Ezekiel 16:20-22, Jeremiah 19:4-5

$\mathcal{M}$y people do not realize that their bodies are Mine. I created them and paid for them through My Son's death on the cross. When My people rebel against Me and make wrong choices, I am there to forgive – but it costs, like you have learned. My creation has order in it. I look for a holy and cleansed body for My Spirit to live in.

1 Corinthians 3:16-17, 6:9-10,
Psalm 53:1, Acts 2:38

*M*y people all want to be loved, but when they worship each other instead of Me, I give them up to their own lusts. Men desire each other and women in the same unnatural ways. This unclean fornication is a horrible sin before Me. Rebellion toward Me leads to immorality – then to violence and murder.

Romans 1:18-29, Leviticus 18:22, 20:13-19, 1 Corinthians 6:9-10

*M*y precious children – you have had a time of hard and heavy words from Me. Drink deeply from the waters of My Spirit. You have been such a comfort to Me! I love you! Since I am a covenant God, what I have is yours – if you give Me what is Mine and the gift of your hearts.

Psalm 60:3, Revelation 22:17, Hebrews 8, Mark 12:30

$\mathcal{C}$ome, My children. I will comfort and refresh you. I will wipe away all your tears over your burden of what lies ahead for the lost. I long to show mercy and grace to My people – if only one person would stand with Me in prayer! Your burden will carry My light to others. Watch Me as I answer your pleas!

2 Corinthians 1:3, Isaiah 28:12-13, Jeremiah 5:1, 31:9,16, Matthew 11:28-30

Oh, My treasures – watch My judgment rush down as falls, bringing forth My righteousness as a mighty stream. Pray that your courts will boast in My commands and serve My people with justice. This is more pleasing to Me than any sacrifice.

Amos 5:24, Proverbs 21:3, Micah 6:8

$\mathcal{L}$ook – there are a few around you who look mighty. Pray that, instead of depending on the pebbles of their own strength, they can put their roots firmly down in Me – the Rock of creation – or the winds of adversity will carry them away. The greatest of your leaders should be a servant to all!

Luke 6:46-49, Isaiah 57:13,
Mark 9:35, Ephesians 3:16-19

*A*lways pray for your country, a land full of promise with its foundation in Me. Give thanks for the freedom I have given you and for those who have sacrificed and are sacrificing their lives for this freedom. Pray daily for them and for your president – for his protection and for wisdom and guidance to serve the people. Pray for those in authority over you.

1 Thessalonians 5:18, 1 Timothy 2:1-3

With spiritual eyes and wings, I will give you the gift of reaching the world to pray. Be prepared to fly out in prayer from your home in Me to where My Spirit sends you. Many of My people are in great pain. Listen to the whispers of My Spirit directing you to pray for someone or call them to pass on a loving word from Me. Be watchful! Be prepared! Listen!

Isaiah 40:1, Matthew 25:13, James 5:13-15

*M*y precious jewels – pray heartily for My people in the churches that they can be united in belief of who I am, who My Son, Jesus, is and what He has done. Pray also for the ongoing work of My Spirit who directs them on their journey toward holiness in Me. I want a glorious Church that walks in unity and power as a warrior Bride for My Son!

John 17, Ephesians 2:11-22, 5:25-30

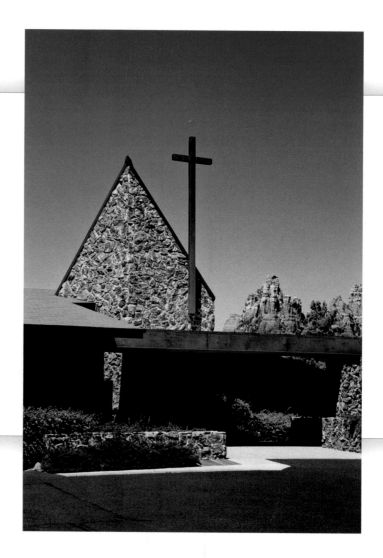

I have gifts for My Church. Pray that My people will be brought into position to humbly and lovingly serve My Church as apostles, prophets, pastors, teachers or evangelists. They will equip and build up My Body, bringing it into maturity and unity of faith in the righteousness of My Son – giving all honor and praise to Him.

Ephesians 4:11-13, Revelation 5:11-14, 1 Corinthians 12:28-31

*O*h, My prayer warriors – in the name of religion, so many of My children have been killed. I have sent prophets and reformers – but hardened hearts, pride, self-righteousness, and man-made rules did away with them. Knowing Me is *not* about ritual or laws, but a life of an intimate loving relationship with Me, your Creator and Lord. My Kingdom has come. Grab ahold of it! Luke 11:2,37-54, James 1:27, Song of Songs

$\mathcal{M}$y children – look at those in My Church who point controlling icy fingers of judgment at each other. This is a rebellious sin and it hurts Me. It stifles My Spirit and I sadly leave. Don't waste the oil My Spirit gives you to keep your "lamps" lit! Pray for tender and forgiving hearts, and for the enemy of your souls to leave.

Matthew 7:1-2, 25:1-13, Proverbs 6:16-19, 1 Thessalonians 5:19, 1 Peter 5:8

$\mathscr{P}$ray, My beloveds, that My people will have the hope of My Son in them. Their lives, like yours, do not need to be ruined by sin. In their pride they think that I cannot forgive them. I am an almighty God whose mercy and love endures forever. Colossians 1:27, Psalms 103:1-5, 107:1-2

*P*ray that My people will call out to Me to break down any walls of sin or addiction between us. I can make them as new babes. As a loving parent, I nurture these babes until they are stilled, quieted, and thoroughly bonded with Me.   Philippians 1:6, Psalms 25:7, 40:1-3, 103:8-14, 131:2, Revelation 21:4-5, Isaiah 49:15-16

*M*y children – your wedding garments, and those for the people in My Church, are prepared for your marriage to My Son. They must have these. Rejoice, for your Bridegroom is coming! Let all know of His invitation to come. Be ready! The wedding supper is prepared! Come!

Matthew 22:1-4, Isaiah 61:10,
Revelation 19:7-9

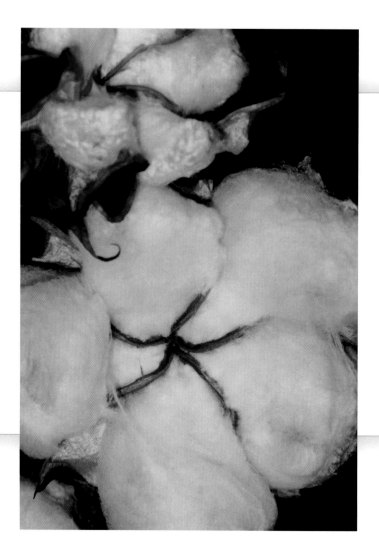

$\mathcal{B}$lessed are you, when you come in My name bringing peace. You, My children, will be clothed in My righteousness and will lighten the countenance of many in darkness. I see your joy working with Me as you watch the impossible come to pass. Continue to fast and pray, My dear ones, and rejoice – for I am with you!

Isaiah 52:7, Luke 18:27, Acts 26:16-18, Ephesians 6:18, Mark 9:29

HEAVEN (REMEMBERING 4-8-68)

Fields where lupine, larkspur and lilies grow,
Mountains of opalescent purple in the distance show
Beauty, brilliant colors of weedless bright patches –
But lo, a picket fence of white sadly snatches
Any frolic in the sun, in the fields –

        along the lanes I want to run.

 What joy, dear Jesus, to sit at Your fiery feet!
As You radiate acceptance and love so sweet.
Rejoice! For I am free from chains of mortality,
The weight of mental fears give place to liberty.
But . . . regretfully, it is not time –

        I am leaving someone behind.

What pain, what agony, what sorrow to return
To heal a splintered, fragmented burdened urn
Shattered by the weight of a steed overturned –
To my little ones who need a guiding hand
And those in need of comfort,

        and those to command.

A taste of freedom, a taste of heaven's pleasures
Pales the siren's call of earth's worldly treasures
And kills the fear and dread of death's dark sting.
To heaven's portals, Jesus, I long to bring
To You a job well done –

        then life's been a battle won.

Denise Park 1982

✝
284

Season 7
Rest

*C*ome unto Me, all ye that labor and
are heavy laden, and I (Jesus) will give
you rest.   Matthew 11:28 KJV

*W*ell done, My faithful servant! You have worked hard. Now it is time for a Sabbath rest – a time for you to joyfully delight in Me and as a sign of My covenant between us. I created the world in six days and rested. Look what we have done together!

Matthew 25:21, Exodus 16:29, 31:14-17, Genesis 1:31, 2:2-3

*M*y child – I have delighted in creating beauty – just for you to enjoy! I hope that through this, you will know that I love you beyond your deepest dream. I am your first and only love. I am a jealous God for you!

Psalms 19:1-6, 57:5, 104:1-34, Revelation 2:4, Deuteronomy 4:24

$\mathcal{M}$y beloved – I call you to rest in Me for times of refreshing and to enjoy the abundant grace I have extended to you. I rejoice that you have overcome much suffering in the world while I drew you to Me, joining our hearts together. Your life will impart a sweet fragrance to those who love Me.   Acts 3:19, 2 Corinthians 1:4, 2:14-16, 1 John 5:4-5, Jeremiah 24:7

I call you blessed among My children. Like these little violets with their faces toward Me, I invite you to enter into My holy Presence and let My love and fragrance envelop you. I want to rejoice over you as a bridegroom rejoices over his bride! When I call you home, I will be there to embrace you.   Psalms 16:11, 115:13, Isaiah 62:5, 2 Corinthians 5:1-8

*T*his will be a winter of rest for you like a butterfly in a cocoon. I will fashion new wings for your life. You have celebrated My delivering you from many chains of bondage in the world. Now it is time to mature and war as My agent in place. You will find rest and safety hidden in My Presence.   Revelation 21:5, Psalms 91:1-2, 116:7, Exodus 33:14

*A*s you hide in My Presence within this secret place in your spirit,
we will review your fruits and blessings of the year and our covenant
together. There we will deepen the bonds of our relationship. I am a
loving God of eternal relationships! Your grateful and passionate heart
lets Mine shower you with wisdom and new revelations of Myself!

Leviticus 23:39-40, Song of Songs, Daniel 2:22, Matthew 13:11

*M*y beautiful creation – let this be a time to draw My Spirit around you and to let your roots grow and be built up in My Word. I delight in your accepting My Word as truth! Seek Me and listen for My voice in the stillness of your spirit and I will give you a glimpse of My glory.

Colossians 2:6-7, John 17:17, Psalms 27:4, 119:2, 1 Kings 19:12

I will give you better understanding of My plans for the rest of your life. You will be fishing among My sheep. I am calling you to nurture them with My gifts and love, which I give you in the time you spend with Me. Trust in My faithfulness and protection toward you.

Jeremiah 29:11, John 21:15-16, Psalms 61:3, 89:8,15

*Y*es, My bride – deeper and deeper
I call you to live in Me. Your heart will be
ravished, as I am your Lover and My
banner over you is love. Even in your
old age when your hairs are white,
I will still care for you. I made you and
I will carry you until I call you home.

Song of Songs 2:4,16, 4:7-9,
Psalms 33:13-15, 37:25, Isaiah 46:4

My child – I am your King who calls you to walk in the riches of My inheritance. I am also calling you to become more like My Son, sharing in His sufferings and glory. I can see the beauty and My gifts in you growing. Keep praying to Me and don't give up! As you honor and give Me glory, I will impart My glorious radiance to you.

Ephesians 1:3-14, 1 Peter 4:13, Isaiah 60:1, Romans 8:29-30, Luke 18:1, Exodus 34:29

$\mathcal{M}$y beautiful child – I am preparing you for what lies ahead. Be ready to press forward as I gently lead you. Thank you for coming on this journey with Me. I see that you are satisfied and feel My rewards.

Philippians 3:13, Matthew 25:21

$\mathcal{I}$ send you a kiss with My blessing and an anointing with My oil of gladness as you finish this work. Go and bless another with My boundless joy and laughter! I love you!   Psalms 45:7, 16:11

Gone Fishing Deeper!

*N*ow unto the King eternal, immortal, invisible, the only wise God, be honour and glory forever and ever. Amen. 1 Timothy 1:17 KJV

The End